sometimes silence
is the space
where love seeps in
& fills its place

after-words

Charlotte Pearl

Roundpond

PRESS

Illustrations and design by Charlotte Pearl.

A CIP catalogue record for this book is available from
the British Library.

www.roundpondpress.com

ISBN: 978-1-3999-4041-2

we need the darkness
of the night
to wonder at
the stars so bright.

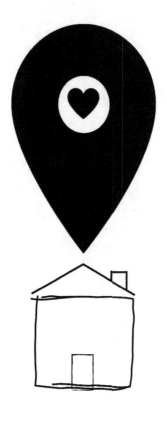

to my family.
My heart is home with you

scribbles

contents

once

escape

self

enough already

love

together in the world

scribbles

once

<u>absconding bees:</u>

When all the bees,
leave the hive.

When staying
isn't safe.

be gentle with your
judgement
here are musings of a heart.
When you've poured
yours out on paper
then pull mine apart

musings

home

Sometimes,
you need to go the wrong way
to find the right way.

Home.

three years old

When I was little, wonder
could be found in the
everyday;
in the way sunshine swallows
shadows whole or snow
transforms shrubs into giant,
white molehills.

snowy morning

I pitter pattered down the stairs
and caught the morning unawares.
Dark had crumbled into light;
a whirling, wilderness of white.
And I saw to my surprise
a snow clad land and snow drenched skies.
What a lovely sight to greet me
from the land of slightly sleepy.

but...
terror can lurk in the
everyday too.

And the 'every-night.'

black ice

Of an evening, when light drew in
and buried itself in darkness,
when cold snapped at branches
of the birch outside our house,
as a swell of smoke slunk
and froze from chimney tops,
we were so snug in the kitchen,
us kids and mum;
a rumpus of nursery rhymes
strained through our din;
happy noise. We didn't want for anything.
All this joy jostling with
silence of smothered streets.
The white seemed infinite but
stumbled footsteps are
a precursor to black ice.
If fear features in your routine
you learn to ostracise foreboding.
The crunch of a gate, the skid of snow,
the slurred profanities
and the children have all gone.
Four small adults, faces and feelings
composed of fear-cold.
You are never too young
to learn 'not to react.'
Whisky fumes herald his invasion.
Hopefully he will pass out tonight.

fairy tales and nursery
rhymes...our interpretation
clouded with childish naivety
we miss their sinister edge.

Unless, of course, life has
keened our vision.

some nursery rhymes
and their meanings

- Ring a ring o' roses - the
  plague
- Mary, Mary quite contrary-
  Bloody Mary, who tortured
  and murdered Protestants.
  Silver bells were
  thumbscrews, cockle shells
  were torture
  devices attached to men's bits
- Ladybird, ladybird- Catholic
  priests burnt at the stake in
  16th century England.
- Lucy Locket- a row between
  two legendary 18th century
  prostitutes.

nursery rhyme

Poor man,
rich man,
broken man, thief.
Steeling laughter
and self belief.

Father,
husband,
bully,
prey.
Love giver, love taker.
Make him go away.

Vodka,
whiskey;
dead-eyed smile.
Singing,
dancing;
safe for a while.

Drunk and slumped and
snoring in a chair.
Tiptoe,
let's go
far from there.

Rich man,
poor man,
broken man,
thief.
We stole back our laughter,
our self belief.

mum shows me an escape
route, that can be reached
without stepping outside.
That opens doors into
dreams and windows into
worlds and lends me wings so
I can fly there. Where letters
are rungs on words to climb
into hearts and minds. Where
I find other things to think
about, to care about, away
from where I am.

school run

When mum took us the little way to school
we didn't walk or run at all.
We rode a horse, then took a train
around the world and back again.
We tamed wild dragons, captured stars,
sometimes re-discovered mars.
We swam through seas where mermaids played
and danced our way through a parade.
We conquered villains, saved the day;
we did a lot that little way.
That little way we had to go;
strange we weren't a little later though.

favourite childhood games

40 40

cops and robbers

kiss chase

stuck in the mud

French skipping

tag

hide and seek

uno

the bailiff game

Shhh now shhh.
Stay quite still.
Duck below the window sill.
Don't make a sound.
Don't say a word.
It's a game.
You can't be heard.
The man outside knocks again,
then looks to leave. I'll tell you when.
And if we're truly sure he's gone
the game is over and we've won!
Until we're sure we'll stay right here,
like two shadows disappear.
Ssh now ssh, keep quiet please do
or he might take your toys from you.

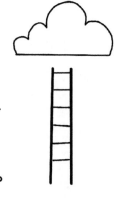

i have learnt that
sometimes
you have to climb
and not look down.

Metaphorically speaking.

bed in the clouds

And when our world became too much
mum caught a cloud to make a bed
and flew us somewhere else instead.
All from the safety of her arms.

scribbles

escape

oh, little caterpillar
I wish that you could see;
inside you hide a butterfly
with wings to set you free

home should be
your safe place.
The place you run to.
Not the place you run from.

one more raindrop

Chaos collects
beneath

the still shimmer,
silence;

water waiting.
Surface

tension spilling,
testing

taught skin stretching –
breaking

as a single
spit

of rain furrows
freedom

in its wake.
Freedom.

the blackness blisters with
imminence, bubbling to a place
past boiling point, jangling our
nerves with the flurry of
fleeing.

I discovered later, Pink Fluff
stayed to guard what was left
behind.

once

There was a girl who knew
that fear could be found
in the slurred scraping of a door key
or a heavy set of footsteps
stumbling up the stairs.
But her mother, whose love made her brave
and whose courage made her strong,
took her and together they tiptoed
in the cloak of night to safety.
To a new home so full of love
that fear could find no place to fit.

the door slams behind us.
We are swallowed into
the safety of night.
Silent, stealthy.
Stowaways
on the number 9 bus.
Afraid to speak
in case he hears us.

For where he lurks
rage rises in his shadow.

it's on them

that's what she said;
the anger that's inside their head,
the pain they put on you instead,
is theirs.
Their rage,
their scars and fears
stored up and strained through
tear stained years,
love's ledger red and in arrears
is theirs.
And once you've tried to listen to
why they do the things they do
and still they take it out on you;
it's theirs.
For after all a words a word,
useless if it isn't heard;
ignore it and it stays absurd;
it's theirs.
Don't give their pain a place to hide,
to settle in, take root inside.
Don't let their pain push out your pride;
it's theirs.
Walk away sew up your heart.
Love hurts but shouldn't from the start.
You know you're better off apart;
it's theirs.

(thing is; there's only so many times until it's yours) .

our knock sounds braver
than we feel and
we enter the shelter.

Here we shield ourselves
in anonymity.
There is victory
in our silence.
Our refusal to give in.
To go back.
We must protect our tribe.
Other mothers and children
hiding
from the outside world.
From all the hims.
Who did this.
To us.

silence

Although I might not say a word
my silence can still be heard.
My silence is loud and true.
Your silence speaks the same for you.

we're boxed up bits
of broken homes
and our memories make
the walls around us.

Everyone here is damaged.
Some
wear it better than others.
Damaged can look scary
when you're small.

forever now

Here we don't have to hide
the chaos happening inside
and yes they've heard it all before;
another mother through the door,
numb dumb with grief too tired to tell
of running from another hell.
Squashed in beds with broken dreams
and sadness stitched along their seams.
Breaths collapse and pile together
in this now that feels forever
but what if I've forgotten how
to smile in this forever now?

things I miss about home

- my friends
- my school
- my bedroom, my bed
- my garden
- space without strangers
- choosing what I want
  to watch on tv
- our nice clean bathroom
- laughing with my friends
  even if I don't feel like it
  until I've forgotten
  I don't feel like it
- my dad

things I don't miss about home

- MY DAD

newness

The problem with newness,
I've come to find,
is new things can't be the old things left behind.
It takes time to love things
when they are all new
until they're like old things that feel part of you.

soon the silence
starts to ask
if it's our victory
or theirs..

our silence sounds like fear.
Theirs says nobody misses us.

So much of me is kept inside,
in the places secrets hide.
Words unsaid stay locked within
the secret chamber of my skin.
And I'm worried I may pop
when secrets fill me to the top.

secrets

time to go.

We are lucky.
My mum's friend knows a
lawyer who can help us.

It won't be easy
and dad will fight us
every step of the way
but we will have a home
and love
and us in it.

breaking

Dawn breaks, new day;
beauty out of disarray.
So much beauty in the making
of this day that's made from breaking.

when I confide in a friend
about the night we swapped
home for a women's refuge
it's as if I'm telling
someone else's story,
as if, I was
a different 'me' then.
But I hadn't chosen
to be brave or strong.
Just to keep going.

**Turns out I'm quite capable
when there is no alternative.**

looking back

I'm so grateful to that refuge
back then I hated it like hell;
too busy being scared to see
who else was scared as well.

<u>scribbles</u>

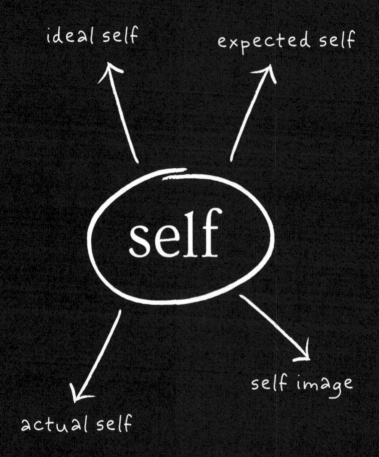

one of the most annoying
phrases ever must be
'are you ok?'
What the asker really means is
'why are you in such a bad
mood?' to which you reply
'I was fine until you asked!'
When what you really mean is
'yes I'm upset
so leave me alone!'
BUT what you really, **really**
want to say is,
'I need a hug.'
Which you do say later when
you've been left long enough
to say
what you REALLY mean.

hedgehog

'my little hedgehog'
mum would say to me,
'how can I hug you
when you're so prickly?'

'Sometimes I'm a hedgehog,
Sometimes I'm a mole,
either I prickle,
or hide in a dark hole.

But if you are patient
and wait a little while
I'll lose all my prickles
and dig out my smile.'

the problem with growing up is
that I want to but I don't. The
 things I was so sure of, when I
was small, have come unstuck.
The things that made me happy
aren't enough anymore. It's
like I'm racing to the part
where EVERYONE knows I've
won.
BUT every now and then
I stop and see
childhood in the distance
and am knocked down
with sadness.

Sometimes,
the most frightening thing
I can be   is me.

being

And when you're afraid that who you are
is not who you want the world to see,
or worse, who the world wants you to be;
consider the sun, how it seeps its warmth into us.
All of us, every one savours the sun.
No pain is new, except, to you.

And anyway the world carries on.
There is a peacefulness in knowing
and waiting and watching and growing
and just being; as light dips down to grey,
as seasons follow come what may.
Who else can we be, except for you and me?

the other thing
about growing up is
all the different boxes
people try to fit you in
along the way.
Or you try out for size.
Sometimes, it's as if
I'm cramming myself
into a space
that doesn't fit.
And then I realise
it doesn't have to.

$$x \div \frac{y^2}{I^2} = y \text{ should } I^2$$

There must be a complicated
algerbraic formulae
to calculate the ratio
of rules to years
you have lived on earth
and the rate at which
the rules
multiply
in correlation to
the number of breaths
you take each day
and what would happen if
you substituted X for Y
when X means
crossing all the boxes
and Y means
Y should I

you are not

the happy homemaker,
the temptress,
the dark horse,
the straight laced swat,
the late night slut,
thicko, wierdo,
frigid, prude,
just plain rude,
the girly girl,
the tomboy,
damaged goods,
sweet and pure,
an optimist,
a pessimist,
the rebel,
the misfit.
The space you fit
is not
a cookie cutter kit,
take your pick
and that's it
for life.

you are

a shape shifter,
life sifter,
species in emergence
moving forwards to a future
that you'll shape along the way.
You are the centre of the universe
that lingers on your fingertips
that links your lungs with trees,
with galaxies;
a fractal pattern on repeat
and yet unique
in a world that finds beauty in numbers
and order in each atom
that binds us all together.
You are an impossible contradiction;
a marvel of geometry,
last week's science fiction,
tomorrow's possibility.

You are your own story
you tell with each rising sun
as new to you as anyone.

and as if it isn't hard enough
already,
I don't know how to feel
about dad.
Angry? Sad???
Do I miss him
or
just miss having a dad?
Is he my perfect excuse
for when I screw up...
or the reason?

And mostly I'm fine.

And anyway, I say I'm fine
because
that's what everyone says.

fine

'How are you?' 'Fine' I say,
when the opposite is true.
But it's easier this way
than spilling out to you.
So I smile away the lie,
disappointed you can't tell.
'And how are you?' I reply.
Oh, you're 'fine' as well.

when dad came home angry
and the air grew thick with words
spat like bullets round us,
I'd make myself quieter,
hunch down and hide.
Occasionally, his attention
turned to me with an
on the spot
times table test.
His ability to calculate
impossible numbers was infinite
and he didn't understand why
I couldn't do
simple multiplications.
Each stammered wrong answer
incited increasing disgust
and worse name calling until I
couldn't speak for fear
of getting it wrong. It's taken
years to learn it's better to try.

shrink me

Once, I tried to shrink myself
to fit into a space small enough
to hide from nasty looks
or unpleasant words.
A soundproof place.
A safe place.
Far away from you.
But far from others too.
Then, when you disappeared
the air around me opened up,
empty of your anger
and your size
and I didn't have to hide.
So I stretched into the open space
and grew.

but sometimes, when the
hurting gets too much or
someone else lets me down.
Or at least
I think they have..
all the nasty things
I've ever heard,
stored up inside me,
squeeze out to sting
someone else instead.

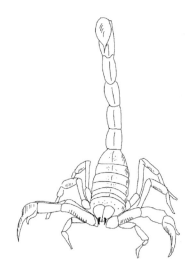

dad

You filled me up
with wicked words
which spill out sometimes
and make me want to
censor myself.
But slowly I'm diluting them.
Diluting you with good things
everywhere around me.
Like a sponge I soak up
small happinesses
and squeeze out the grime.
And there will be a time
life will wring me through
and water will run clear. Of you.

and later
when the hurting fades
I'm left silent and ashamed.

after-words

Those words I whispered, mumbled, stuttered,
if only they had stayed un-muttered.
They really were just that, just words,
that you happen to have heard.
But now they're hanging in the air
and you just happened to be there.

or I may speak a bit too fast
or laugh a bit too loudly
to fill the space
he left behind.
But when I can't
gather the energy
to do either
and would rather disappear
from inquisition,
I hide in my room
and wish my mum would just
understand without
me telling her how I feel.

And wish she wouldn't come
and check on me.

But I'm glad she does.

origami

Sometimes I wish I could fold in on myself
until I made something else.
All my angles and my edges
snipped and clipped like shapes in hedges,
clicked and clacked to something new,
hidden from your point of view;
 a transformer I'd become
something more than this someone.

mum,

there are times;

my head is full with being me
and all the things I want to be
and all the things I want to do
and all of them away from you.

It doesn't mean
I dont love you.
I just need quiet
to hear myself think,
to work out who I am,
not who you think I should be.

'you've changed'

Why when you say 'you've changed',
in a voice quiet enough
to make me listen louder,
does it hit me in the heart
like fully loaded word ammo?
No need to elaborate,
disappointment puckering
your forehead fills in the blanks.
Changed. FOR THE WORST.
Yet stories pushed through screens
like Oscar winning scripts
call change a celebration.
Strangers sit and stare
at transformations daily;
rags to riches, fat to fit.
Tales of small successes
fuel our inspiration.
But not this time.
This change is a let down;
a put down
that prickles my conscience
and challenges my sense of self
into being someone else;
a reflection of how you wish the world to see me.
But maybe, just maybe, you need to change
and accept I'm not another you;
that I'm my own person too.

but then you surprise me
with your belief in
what I **can** do
and your belief
gives me wings.

Flutter by butterfly,
life is not what it seems
so take to the sky
and follow your dreams

give your thoughts wings

Shake out the thought
and there it is
a thing with wings
that can become
something done.
That part of me
is loosed and free
not locked up hiding in my head;
it's busy being said instead.

although
you need to know
it's not enough to say
'some things
don't make sense,'
as if that is the answer

And I argue because I doubt myself.
I'm cross in case
what you've told me isn't true;
in case you've lived a lie
and made me your auxiliary.
I raise my voice to rile you
into convincing me
my foundations are steady.
If I stop shouting
the space in your silence
says too much.
Perhaps when I'm older,
I'll accept as you do;
worn down by questions
we can't answer.
Until then,
I'll continue
to challenge us both.

questions

and another thing; parents
moan about moody teenagers
but they know
how this works...
Maybe I'm irrational
but I have a great excuse;
HORMONES...remember??!!!
So leave me to my silence
in the mornings.
Don't crack
snide comments about
my conversational skills.
We both know where it will
lead. Sometimes I'm angry.
Full stop. So, well... **stop**.
Leave me alone.
Don't follow me
and ask if I'm okay.
I want to be miserable
without you ruining it.

sorry

Sorry.
Not sorry really.
Can't help it.
Wont say it.
Don't feel it.
Should say it.
Won't be it.
It's just
you're ....
SO annoying
and I don't want to
think about you
or what you feel.
You're my mum;
you need
to just
take it.
Get it.
Be there.
Here.

Oh. You are.
Sorry.

but with you
I'm never scared you'll
leave.
And wherever I may be,
And no matter how sad
or angry I am
I know I can come back to
you.
And you will
fold me into your arms.
And everything will be okay.

Because
your heart is a house
which I call home.

You will never be alone.
I can always bring you home

maybe because of
'everything'
I'm good at guessing
how others feel and

it's amazing
what you hear and see
when you stay still
and be.

just because

People say things just because,
because they sound like things to say
but what is unsaid matters more
if you listen long enough

i think some people *like*
feeling sorry for others.
It makes them feel better
about themselves.
And it annoys them to see
someone surviving,
worse still,
triumphing
with grace, dignity
and chutzpah
because they know
they never could.

mum

People have preconceived ideas
about what life looks like
painted on a person's face.
Agony and grief rendered
in shades of grit and grey.
Oppression and survival
depicted in charcoal and desolation.
They find it offensive when
the subject dares to beguile
in a sunset's multicoloured blaze;
descending in glory
ready to rise another day.

but I have noticed that
sometimes the people
you least expect
bring the most unexpected
happinesses.

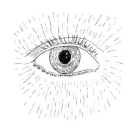

stranger

Sometimes it takes a stranger
to cut through
the silence of our brooding,
and remind us that
we are not alone in our worries.
Someone you have never met before
who overcomes
the vastness of improbability,
the vastness of this world,
to meet you in the moment.

and I have noticed that
some people
hide parts of themselves,
to fit in.
That hiding ourselves
is something we learn
alongside our a,b,c

And the truth is,
even I
don't always know
who I'm going to
wake up and get.
Sometimes I dream
of falling in love
and sometimes
I'm a feisty feminist
who doesn't need a man
to make her happy.

janus

Do you know what it is
to co-exist with yourself?
Balancing the outside you,
the world sees,
with the inside you
that waits and hides.

Do you know what it is
to be someone's someone else?
so carefully self-curated,
so far from your full stop
starting point the details disappear.
Do you know what it is
to navigate who you should be
and who you are?

What if Janus had spun around;
if past and future had faced off?
Destiny and history colliding,
disappearing in confusion.
I am tired of ignoring who I am
and scared I can't find who I was.
But more afraid of losing
everything built on my better me.

what makes me sad though
are the times when
I'm not brave enough
to be the me
I'm most proud of.

the facts

You can't fast track, zoom back,
amplify or magnify time racing by.
Skip past the drag in real-time lag,
erase the blips and jump the dips.

It doesn't work that way.

You're a compound, profound,
mixed array of night and day,
ups and downs, smiles and frowns,
inbetween-ers, non stop screamers,
the things you think and say and do.
The bits and bobs of being you.

And they're the facts.

but...all of this staying
and moping is
boring .
I'm itchy wondering
what fun
I'm missing out on .

tiptoeing

We weren't born to live just the big moments,
the sad moments, the soft moments,
those small in between moments,
the ones you wait a lifetime for
that don't live up to time wasted waiting. Moments.

We were born to live them all.

Each monumental, minuscule,
complex cosmos fill of moments
that compound and contract
into this fact of being.
Oh, it's a very busy business is this being.

But it keeps us on our toes.

♡ 3

an almost wish

I almost wish smart phones
hadn't been invented.
The more I post and snap
and comment and like,
the more I'm sure
I'm missing out.

more

Before I knew enough to question more,
before growing up meant being more,
before noticing meant wanting more,
before a night out meant doing more,
before all that I didn't NEED more.

it's hard to ignore what
other people are up to
and be happy home instead.
Even if you don't feel like
you're missing out
it's easy to feel **left** out
when all you have to do
is look at your phone
and see smiling faces
without you.

Sometimes we are wild
and free.
And sometimes
we just stay and be

no plans

Every day does not need to echo
with the excess of exuberance
or each night fill to bursting
with people and places.
Don't hold yourself to ransom with
fun as task master and reward
or fear that if you stop
your world stops with you.
Sometimes we need to
steel ourselves to stillness;
stop to unscramble our ideas
from high frequency opinions.
Revelations can linger
in the soft silences
when nothing might be
the greatest something you can do.

BUT when,
the world catches me
unawares,
forcing me with
it's impossible beauty
to watch with such wonder
that there is no room for
anything else; in that moment all
worries, are pushed out and
replaced with hope for what is
possible.
I think it might be
a type of prayer,
this pulsed thought of thanks
for being part of such a 'now'.

I want to fill jam jars with this
feeling to spread on greyer days

breathe

Little bit, by little bit I tiptoe into the moment.
With slow wonder I watch day arrive
through the chink of an early morning;
survey it spread across the street, the hill,
the world beyond.
Unwrinkled, unblemished, as yet un-done.

Purpose presses. Possibility persuades.
Softly, so softly light leaks in
so as now can see it's way past then.
I take now by it's corners
and shake it out before me.
Birds burst forth and stipple the silence.
A rising hymn. Let the day begin

b r e a t h e

and you never know
when the world
will show its upper hand

stardust

When the earth bore down on its bones
dust turned to diamonds
and glittered in the darkness.
When the world weighed down on you
the stars sparkled through your skin
and the darkness
showed you how brightly you can shine.

scribbles

enough
already

when I've had enough of rain
I sit & wait for sun again

i'm too old to believe in magic.
At least that's what I tell
myself. But whatever you
might call it, each time I've felt
at my lowest it's as if the world
has sent a signal that
everything will be ok. More
than that; there is life to be
lived and it is wonderful.

another blossom tree

it was cold and it was dark.
At least
I think that's how the weather was
when I walked around the corner
and saw
just another blossom tree,
in one small spot of sun,
waiting for me there like that;
a wish,
a promise,
an answer
to all the grey around.

i saved my own life
by walking away.
But I wasn't all strength.
There were times I fell
and got myself up
and wondered

what if
it was me
 and not you?

burn out

'Stop waiting to be wanted.
Relinquish rhetoric that states
blood is thicker than water.
Believing that will drown you with indifference.'
I shut my eyes and wish a lie of love.
You were the star, my heart the soft focus filter...
But all stars burn out
and by then you had pushed me
far from the explosion.

i'm an optimist.
I don't want to believe the
worst of anyone, or anything.
I think that helps - knowing
it will get better. And
generally **it** does. But when **it**
doesn't, when people just
aren't 'better' like they
should be, it hurts so much
more.

rainbows

Although you feel fragmented,
although the day is grey;
light also leaks through
the cracks in the clouds.
Gather your fragments and
refract each ray into rainbows.

some people hate the dark.
I don't mind it at all. As
long as I feel safe, I like
the silence and space to
think but sometimes I wish
I could switch thoughts
off when I'm ready to
sleep.

Once I spent the whole
night trying to get to sleep
and the whole next day
trying to stay awake.

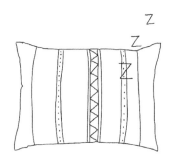

4am thoughts

Stirring, whirring, wizzing, stop.
Brittle thoughts fizz & pop.
Worries whisked into a frenzy,
reasons running round inside me;
curbing sleep with profound
doubts and questions whooshing round
the solid stealth of 4am.
Wait for light to leak again:
erase my fickle fears away
with the bright hindsight of day.

when I was little I thought the
world would seem smaller, the
more I grew. But it's the
opposite. As I get bigger the
world gets bigger with me. The
older I am the more there is
to see, to do, friends to
make, happinesses I hadn't
even dreamt of.

And the unbearable grief
of losing loved ones .

grief

We push grief out
with words and things.
As many things
as we can fit
into the space
where grief might sit.
We push grief out
until the time
it grows too big;
it pushes through
the parts of you
held in reserve
and eats you up
and spits you out
and you don't know
where it will stop.
Until it does.
And then you miss
the grief because
it's gone.

And still the grief has won.

And that's what grief does.

i am fine until I'm not.
I'm so good at showing
everyone else how okay I am
often I dupe myself in the
process.

I had to stop today.

Take a b r e a t h.

Hold it until
I stemmed
the overspill

of words and thoughts
and worries brewing,
of all the do's and don'ts
of doing.

I thought I was fine.

Just goes to show,
what do I know?

overspill

then I need to escape and
walk and walk until I walk
away from feeling bad.
And if it's raining and
thundering sometimes
that's good too because
the storm is out and then
it's gone.

let it rain

There is a delicious sense of rebellion
that comes with walking in the rain.
Head bare. I don't care.
Coat askew. Wet right through.
Drops drip from nose to lip.
People stop to look and tut
from underneath the glut
of low lying, pavement vying
umbrella clouds that
strut the street.

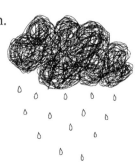

Sloshing feet shuffle on or watch me from
a shop awning, frown dawning
at this wilful act of wild abandon;
disapproving, lips not moving
and looks convey the words they'd say;
'you'll get a cold!' But I'm too old to be told.
Lorry driver do your worst and screech on through
the puddles too;
spraying me. Can't you see?
Wet hair. I don't care.

...Still not there.
...Brrr.

some things you learn
make your thoughts
flip flop.
I heard that
when it comes down to it,
we are really just
a sackful of particles.
So why does living
hurt so much?

the point ●

There comes a point when;
a thought is no profounder
the more that you think on it.
When pain does not deepen
the more that you dwell on it.
When in fact, nothing more can be done by you,
nothing more can be done to you
and so be it.

There comes a point when;
the worst happens and
you can't see how it gets better.
When you can't fix
what is broken
and yes! Your heart seems in pieces
rattling round inside of you
and yet. And yet.

Despite all this,
the sharpness of your breadth
reminds you that you're breathing still
and look!
See how a small slice of moon
shines bright enough to split the darkness.
Never mind she isn't whole.
Just now.

There is hope in this realisation.
And that is the point.

some facts about time

- time can't keep track of itself (there's hope for me yet)
- when dinosaurs were alive there were 370 days in a year
- the faster you move the slower time passes
- time passes faster for your face than your feet (so unfair- I'd much rather have older feet)
- we are looking at the past. When you see the sun it is already 8 minutes, 20 seconds old because of the time it takes for light to reach us

time

There's no wrong time or right time,
your time or my time;
the thing about time
is it never stays still.
Whatever we're doing
it ticks by regardless,
so live it with love
and do what you will.

RANT

I cried and cried when I first got my period. I wasn't ready to grow up. But life is what makes you grow up. Not a bit of blood. That's just a body doing what a body does. No, NO, it's not just 'doing what a body does;' it's actually a remarkable mechanism for making sure the human race doesnt die out. They can also be painful, inconvenient, too long, too short or absent. So STOP with the stupid jokes. Boys.

red

Red the colour of love,
as in my heart is beating wildly for you.
The heart; that vital organ
pumping life blood round your body.
Red as in irony, like that bunch of roses
drooping with the burden of their offering,
strewn in a black bucket of water,
soaked in the fumes of a garage kiosk.
Red as in the the colour of passion,
of disappointment,
of fury.
Red as in danger dancing in plain site,
telling us to stop before something goes wrong.
Red as in blood, as in war, as in glory, as in honour,
as in shame; the colour of your cheeks
seeping up into your eyes and burning them with its hot guilt.
Red the colour of heat.
Pouring out of you,
soaking you in the colour of
love, irony, passion, disappointment,
fury, danger, glory, honour,
shame, guilt, heat,
blood.
Until it's shadow is branded on the very clothes you wear.
On your soul. Your sex.
Your heart;
That vital organ.
Red as in the life blood of
the next generation.

i know I am small
in the eyes of the world.
And why should I care about
something so stupid when
there are all the other worthy
worries going on every day.
But it's difficult to ignore
something
that's the main thing
anyone seems to talk about.

Looks and other superficial
stuff like that.

balanced life

Perfect face and perfects tits
take work and dedication;
If you want happy bits
take up meditation.
If only perfection
had a quicker fix...
Life is about balance;
I'll have salad with my chips.

it seems I spent so much time
devising ways to get through
school;
concocting excuses for being
late, missing homework,
moaning about early
mornings and homework,
that I never stopped to think
how I'd feel when it.
 Stopped.
Last assembly, last lesson,
last bell.
Last filing out of the school
gates.

Forever.

the last school bell

No matter how much you want them
all endings come with sadness.
Sometimes relief, often excitement
but always sadness.
We can't help it. We are creatures of habit.
We depend on routine to tune out the unknown,
lost until we find the replacement.
The day the school bell rang for the last time
we fizzed from the gates like shaken up champagne.
Drunk on freedom.
Later we'd be drunk on cheap spirits and beer.
Shirts graffitied. Love notes from friends we almost made,
from teachers whose skills surpassed salaries.
We ran round giddy with possibility.
Excited. Sad. Scared
School's out. Time for the replacement.

climbing

I'll take the troubles of today.
I'll take the heartache of the night.
I'll spread them out and let them breathe.
I'll tell myself that it's alright
to cry and sob and cry again
until my tears cascade like rain,
until my grief pours itself dry,
until there's no tears left to cry.

And when I've washed and dried my heart
and when I'm bored of staying still
and when I'm strong enough to start
I'll take my strength and climb the hill.
For there's a time to grieve and rest.
For healing hurts and it takes time.
But I am told the view is best
when you are ready for the climb

scribbles

i wasn't waiting for love
when I fell in love with you.

No that's a lie.

Iv'e been waiting for a while.
For someone to love me.
Completely
and know me inside out.

And still love me.

Like I love you.

making out

Words tiptoe on my tongue;
all the things I want to tell you.
How it feels like remembering, being with you,
because I can't imagine us apart.
How heavy the hours are
when you're not here.
How everything that matters
disappears when you smile.
How much it scares me to love strongly,
to love softly.
How I hope that you don't like me
because you're too kind not to.
But I can't risk saying them,
so I stockpile them instead
and we make out.

turns out you don't want
to
love me completely.

Just partially,
when it suits you,
on your own terms.
Which seems to mean
you have time
to 'love' other girls too.

So why, why, WHY do I still
want to be with you???

Couldn't you just grow boils
or something helpful?!

missing kissing

Where do kisses go
when lips no longer meet?
Do they linger in the air
and saunter down the street?
I know the love that put them there
can't just disappear;
where do kisses go
when love's no longer here?

they said we weren't right
together. Don't **they** know
saying that doesn't take
away the hurt?
In fact it makes it worse,
knowing **everyone** realised
we were a disaster
except for me.

to an almost ex.

Why are you so loveable?
Why are you so huggable?
It makes it so improbable
that you could be this horrible.

but love doesn't disappear
because it hurts.
Or because it doesn't make
sense.
Or because other people tell
you it's wrong.
You can't care so much for
someone then dissect their
happiness from yours.
It's not a medical procedure.
The best you can hope for is
that one day you wake up
and love's morphed into
missing.

not knowing you

When we first met
I wished I'd known you sooner
not to miss any of you.
Now I wish I knew you still.
Because you are gone.
And I don't know you at all.

although...
the world is a big place
and it's filled with people.
So many someones
still to meet
who might just
be

the one

THE ←

1

off

It turns out that
love has a sell by date.
If you leave it on the shelf for too long
even love goes off.

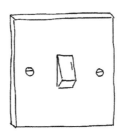

and there is someone new
I like
a lot.
Who likes me.
I think.
Possibly
a lot.
We've been
seeing each other
a lot.
I won't call it love.
But I don't know
what else to call it.
Some nameless feeling
I hope stays with me forever.

opt in ☑

If you shut your eyes
to hide from the dark
you won't see the stars
that light up the sky.
If you close your heart
to not get hurt
you won't find love
that lights you up.
Life is not a multiple choice;
tick the best bits,
leave out the rest.
Living is an opt in all,
wonder, pain, love, the lot.

some people won't like you
as you are.
Some people will.

It's knowing
where to find the right ones

self definition

Because someone loves you
does not mean they know how to be you,
or can remember for you,
or make decisions on your behalf.
Love should give you
the strength to believe in yourself,
encourage you to take second chances
by helping you make first chances happen.
And anyway, at some point
you will have to stand on your own two feet.
And be your own self-definition.
And real love will cheer you on.

it is winter and darkness
clings to the corners of the
sky. I set off for hockey
training and pull the door
behind me. I'd much rather be
in bed.
I speed up to outrun the cold
and sink into the rhythm of
stomping and silence and
being by myself. And then
somewhere between home and
halfway there I think that
maybe, sometimes, it's nice
not to need anyone else.
Breathe in, breath out.
Stand up tall and feel free.

stomping

Sometimes stomping through
the morning dew
that rises up like backwards rain
reaching for the skies again,
watching how
the grass blades bow
beneath your feet
in mock defeat,
can start your day
a different way
than if you stayed
at home afraid
of what might be
or what might not.
Sometimes stomping
helps a lot.

but eventually
optimism dries up.
No-one's glass stays
half-full forever.

I didn't want to risk
'I love you.'
But you did
when I needed it most.

What if glass half-full
isn't the better option?
An empty one
can be filled with love.

lifeguard

It's funny how a little thing
like your hand holding mine
feels like you've pulled me from the sea
and saved me just in time.

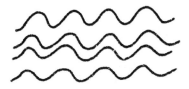

you are my everything
(you know who you are)

me and you

The sun will still shine in the morning...
or not, as the case may be.
The days will still carry on dawning
irrespective of you or me.
So lay your sweet head down this evening.
Summon your strength anew.
For as long as we are still breathing
we can take on the world; me and you.

scribbles

together
in the world

when I worry people will notice me for doing or saying the wrong thing, for standing out, not in a good way, mum reminds me that most people are far too busy with their own worries to notice mine. And then my thoughts pan out from me, to the people around me, to the world around them and I realise she's right.

ordinary

It commenced an ordinary day
which is what made its unravelling so
extra-ordinary. I guess.
The greyness dropped down from the sky,
dank and heavy and met
dirty pavements without a thud.
People marched about their business,
their efforts etched upon their faces.
Swaying through the smog.
Wading their way in waves.
Thoughts rising.
Quiet secrets that make up a life.

but how much nicer it would
be if we did
all pay more attention.
Noticed each other more.
Not to put each other down.
But to help each other up.

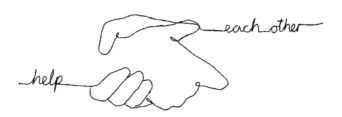

we

All of us busy just getting on,
sidestepping where the other has gone.
All of us lost in what we must do,
lost in our thoughts about I and not you.
But sometimes a thought is better off said
than scared and alone inside of your head.
And maybe, just maybe, people will see
we're better off thinking "we" and not "me"

and I think that's what I miss
about school most.
A group of people put
together who for the most
part, get on.
Because they **have** to.

And then,
because they **want** to.

mind maps

Imagine what we'd see
if imprints of our minds could be
left where others walked before.
if all our thoughts and many more
were flung together reaching high
to build a tower to the sky
of lives that cross and overlap,
ploughing on or racing back.
For wherever you have been
someone else has been and seen;
taking out their joys or pain
to wash away with morning rain.

unravelling a rainbow
part 1

So colour is an illusion.
It's only real inside our heads.
If we shut our eyes
this technicolour triumph
does not exist outside our imagination.
What does exist is light.
What does exist is us.
A collaboration with our eyes,
an interpretation by our brains
and we have manufactured a figment of imagination
powerful enough
to navigate our way,
pinpoint our place in life
enhance our everyday.
Don't tell me we're not sensationalist.

unravelling a rainbow

part 2

And if colours are made up of light
so all colours are one and the same;
unified as a rainbow
seen from a different point of view.
Therefore the existence of one colour
implies the existence of all others.

I wish a rainbow of peoples;
the same yet different;
Individuals who can work as one .

it's really quite remarkable
all the facts that have to
come together
just so we can breathe

miracle

There is no nothingness.
All the little atoms run around and meet
and make something new.
And that is something.
It is a miracle

i wish kindness would spread
like butter on bread

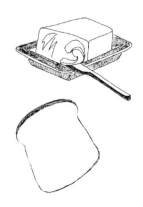

kindness

With kindness you are a sorcerer,
conjuring happiness from nowhere,
strength from somewhere.

A little something;
a word, a touch, a smile,
can be everything.

Such strange magic this kindness;
to change a lifetime.
In a moment.

and everyone kept saying
how important it was that we
work together to defeat this
microscopic organism that
was threatening our lives.

coronavirus

You can't contain a people,
a species, a human population.
You can't order it.
Segregate it into sections
like some kid's prized collection.
Dissect us down
we're all four types of atoms.
And anyway, not so clever
to keep to your category now, is it?
But why trade wisdoms
when we can trade weapons. Huh?
Walls won't work with nature
but breaking boundaries will.
Togetherness is what it takes.
And to think a thing so small
should show us where our strength lies.

but the headlines
didn't change.
And keeping our distance
meant the quiet voices
sometimes disappeared
completely.

sonority

So speak your silence.
Let your beating heart
become the baseline of your song
and send it spinning
in the space between us.
Let words reach out
where we may not.

For someone, somewhere
is stretching in their stillness
to hear hope
and if we all sing out together
we'll make noise enough
to know we're not alone.

thoughts on lockdown

and we baked more biscuits
and sewed more seeds
and tie dyed t-shirts
and they were fun for a bit.
Days on repeat.
But then
I worried my friends had
forgotten me
as we locked each other out
and sunk into hibernation.
And the headlines spewed out
an ever bigger death toll from
the corner in the kitchen, on a
radio more used to cheesy pop.
And I worried about a future
with no exams to qualify my
years at school.

sing out

And all the while we were
locked away with our worries
wondering if we were the only ones
who felt this way.
Too scared to see anyone
and too scared to say anything.

And then
we saw them singing in Italy
on the news at teatime,
across the balconies,
along the streets;
their words met
and broke the silence
and saved us all.
And soon everyone was singing.
And clapping.
And touching hearts
without touching hands.

but when I looked outside,
the sky seemed to breathe
bigger, widened without
the constant car fumes
and the blue deepened
and filled with birdsong.
And we all knew it shouldn't
take something so bad
to give our planet a chance.

what we can do

Even if it's me and you,
if all the me's and you's act too
think how much we can do.
Just with me and you.

press pause ⏸

Press pause on the day.
Press pause on this minute.
On the breathe of this moment.
On the clock that is ticking
off seconds
of time unobserved,
of dreams dropped and lost
of a season that slips past
whilst no one is watching,
too busy waiting
whilst outside my window
a swallow is cutting
the blue with its' path
and a blossom tree blazes
a riot of white
and the sun is now dropping
into the night
Despite pressing pause.

And now is extending
into forever.
Or so it seems to us,
the days are all one to us.
But the chicks in the nest
have hatched and are calling.
No nature's not stalling.
And they do not know
what life has in store
they just chirrup more.
But somehow we lost
desire to notice,
our eagle eye focus
on what is around us.
But slow motion found us
and then it rewound us.
And while we've been slowing
the world is still going.
For the art of just being
is looking and seeing.
It's rather like praying
this seeing and staying

I wrote this one for me.
And for you.

you

You are born you;
and the world enters.
Gradually;
a little less you,
a little more them,
Until.
You are old enough to know
you were enough before.

so this is goodbye...almost
I hope you've enjoyed reading
it.
I feel good to have written it.
Like I've emptied myself out
ready to stock up on tomorrow
and all the tomorrows.

Tired but good.
.

It's 2 am
And time to sleep.

I want to wake up smiling.
So I think I just might.

clearing up

Take off your fear,
hang it up by the door.
Wash off your pretence
and the worry you wore.
Pack away the desire
to prove you're alright.
Let safe conversations
swim away in the night.
Fold up formality
onto the shelf
And then just like that
you are left with yourself.
And then just like that
you are wonderfully free.
Because home is the heartbeat
where you can just be.

recycle

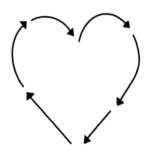

Bask in the sunshine of a smile.
Let it warm you up a while.
But afterwards do your bit;
remember to recycle it!

Please do your bit and
pass this book on to
anyone who might like it

let's chase our dreams
and see where they take us...